MW00681205

HOLLYWOOD LOVERS

EDITED BY J.C. SUARES

THOMASSON · GRANT

Published by Thomasson-Grant, Inc.

Copyright © 1994 J. C. Suarès.
Captions copyright © 1994 J. Spencer Beck.

Printed in Hong Kong.

ISBN 1-56566-058-7

00 99 98 97 96 95 94 5 4 3 2 1

Inquiries should be directed to:
Thomasson-Grant, Inc.
One Morton Drive, Suite 500
Charlottesville, Virginia 22903-6806
(804) 977-1780

Errol Flynn (with Olivia de Havilland)
THE ADVENTURES OF ROBIN HOOD, 1938

John Gilbert and Rudolph Valentino, Clark Gable and Cary Grant, Tom Cruise and Richard Gere. Was there ever a real-life lover as good as the screen gods manufactured by MGM and Warner Bros., Columbia and Paramount?

The movies can be a powerful aphrodisiac, a fact that Hollywood has banked on from its earliest silent-screen days. For over seventy-five years, movie fans the world over have pined away in the dark as their favorite celluloid lovers have fueled their wildest fantasies and most erotic dreams.

Of course, everybody's fantasy is different, and the collective Hollywood love machine has churned out screen lotharios in a startling array of types: slender, exotic Latin lovers Valentino and Ramon Novarro; strapping he-men Clark Gable and John Wayne; charming and sophisticated William Powell and Cary Grant; and shy and sensitive Montgomery Clift and James Dean.

So what makes a great screen lover? As in real life, the answer isn't always skin-deep. Gable's ears are too big, Tom Cruise is below average in height, and Humphrey Bogart is borderline unattractive. Masculinity in the traditional sense often has little to do with it. Tyrone Power is a bit *too* pretty, Montgomery Clift a little *too* sensitive. How about youth? That's certainly not the case when you consider the careers of Cary Grant or Gary Cooper, both of whom continued to seduce their on-screen leading ladies well into their fifties.

Then, too, life has a way of imitating art in Tinseltown, and when *reel* life spills over into real life, the fantasy becomes palpable. There is a reason why Gable and Joan Crawford heat up the screen in so many 1930s movies. They were lovers off the set as well. And who couldn't help but feel that the passion between Elizabeth Taylor and Richard Burton in *Cleopatra* was real? (It was!) So intense was the attraction between the great Garbo and John Gilbert during the filming of *Flesh and the Devil*, the director was too embarrassed to yell "Cut!" after one particularly smoldering scene. He simply walked off the set, leaving the two lovers to carry on privately.

But real-life animal magnetism doesn't always explain the explosive on-screen chemistry between two stars. No, a great screen lover must have something else. Perhaps that elusive quality can best be described simply as "it." Some have "it," and others don't. Call it star quality, if you will, or charisma. And maybe it's partly our own wishful thinking. But when the camera falls in love with Gable or Barrymore, Newman or Redford, so do we.

Rudolph Valentino (with Agnes Ayres)
THE SHEIK, 1921

*Rodolfo Alfonzo Raffaele Pierre Philibert Guglielmi di Valentino
d'Antonguolla, aka Valentino, seduced Agnes Ayres in his biggest-
grossing film and millions of women the world over with his brooding
sensuality and unattainable exoticness. Nearly seventy years after
his untimely death, the former gardener, thief, gigolo, and dancer
is still the archetype of the screen lover.*

Douglas Fairbanks (with Mary Astor)
DON Q., SON OF ZORRO, 1925
The not-very-tall son of a prominent Jewish attorney,
Hollywood's original swashbuckler won women by his smiling
exuberance and sheer physical prowess (professional stuntmen imitated
him). When Fairbanks married fellow silent star and real-life love
Mary Pickford in 1920, Hollywood royalty was born.

Franchot Tone (with Joan Crawford)
DANCING LADY, 1933
Charming, intelligent, and urbane—on-screen and off—
Tone may have lost his costar in Dancing Lady *to the decidedly more*
plebeian Clark Gable, but Crawford opted for
sophistication over animal magnetism in real life and married Tone
when both men proposed marriage in the early '30s.

Robert Montgomery (with Joan Crawford)

FORSAKING ALL OTHERS, 1934

*Happy-go-lucky and self-effacing Montgomery was the perfect foil
for such glittering and egomaniacal 1930s stars as Crawford,
Garbo, and Shearer. Like Franchot Tone, the handsome actor gets
dumped by Crawford for Gable in* Forsaking All Others;
*unlike Tone, Montgomery was able to segue into directing when
his leading-man days waned by the '40s.*

11

John Barrymore (with Joan Crawford)
GRAND HOTEL, 1932
Stage-trained scion of America's leading acting clan,
The Great Profile wooed audiences (but not tough-girl Crawford
here) by his magnificent eloquence and camera-perfect face.
Critic Heywood Broun once remarked:
"He moved through a movie scene like an exquisite paper knife."

John Barrymore (with Greta Garbo)
Grand Hotel, 1932

*After twenty years of film stardom, Barrymore still made
fans swoon when his debonair jewelry thief in* Grand Hotel *confesses
undying love for the languorous ballerina Grusinskaya, played by
Garbo. But fifty years old and increasingly dissolute from years of
drinking, the most famous Barrymore next played a drunken,
has-been actor in* Dinner at Eight, *underscoring the real-life
dilemma of many an aging screen lothario.*

Ramon Navarro (with Greta Garbo)
MATA HARI, 1931 (ABOVE)

Shadowed by Valentino's fame throughout the silent era, the one-time singing waiter from Durango, Mexico, shone briefly in the "talkies" when he seduced the enigmatic Mata Hari—and audiences everywhere—by the film's end.

John Gilbert (with Greta Garbo)
LOVE, 1927 (RIGHT)

Valentino's only true contender for greatest screen lover during the silent era, the dashing Gilbert made four blockbusters with Garbo for MGM, whose pre-Hays-Code publicity machine shrewdly fueled exaggerated rumors of the celluloid couple's off-screen romance. Of the idols who toppled with the coming of sound, Gilbert, with his tinny voice, fell most tragically, dying in drunken despair at the age of 41.

Robert Taylor (with Greta Garbo)

CAMILLE, 1937

With his "perfect profile" and impressive widow's peak,
Robert Taylor's beauty almost outshines the great Garbo's
in one of Hollywood's most romantic movies. The husband of
Barbara Stanwyck and durable leading man (he was under
contract with MGM for 25 years, longer than any other star),
Taylor possessed a made-for-MGM glamour that more than
compensated for his admittedly meager acting talent.

Gary Cooper (with Marlene Dietrich)
MOROCCO, 1930 (ABOVE)

Although the all-American Cooper tangled with Morocco's impossibly Teutonic director (Josef von Sternberg), his brief off-screen romance with his tempting leading lady was decidedly more gemütlich. On-screen, the actor's youthful prettiness (helped along by some heavy makeup) and slightly effete mannerisms were a perfect and arousing foil for Dietrich's fascinating androgyny.

Cary Grant (with Mae West)
SHE DONE HIM WRONG, 1933 (RIGHT)

Urbane—but never snobbish—the self-invented aristocrat born Archie Leach charmed Depression-era audiences after the screen's original liberated lady, Mae West, insisted the handsome newcomer costar with her in her first Hollywood film. In a gender-bending reversal, West is the leading man in She Done Him Wrong *and Grant the prize catch, cajoled by La West with the immortal line: "Come up and see me sometime!"*

Ronald Colman (with Myrna Loy)
THE DEVIL TO PAY, 1930 (ABOVE)

Born to lower-middle-class English parents like his successor
Cary Grant, Colman ironically made his mark playing polished
aristocrats, as he did in this light drawing-room comedy, featuring a
relatively unknown (and very blonde!) Myrna Loy. One of only a
handful of stars who enjoyed popularity in both silent and sound
pictures, the suave Colman ended his ten-year association with
Samuel Goldwyn in 1933 after the latter reportedly accused
the actor of always getting drunk before his love scenes.

William Powell (with Myrna Loy)
THE GREAT ZIEGFELD, 1936 (RIGHT)

Middle-aged and not conventionally handsome, the ex-husband of
Carole Lombard and fiancé of Jean Harlow was nevertheless at the
height of his career in 1936, appearing in Ziegfeld *(the year's*
Best Picture), My Man Godfrey, *and* Libeled Lady—
all hits. Having already won popular acclaim in their
Thin Man *series, the charismatic Loy-Powell duo proved*
that married screen lovers can have fun too.

Clark Gable (with Myrna Loy and Joan Crawford)
MANHATTAN MELODRAMA, 1934 (ABOVE)
POSSESSED, 1931 (RIGHT)
*A rake with a heart of gold, on-screen and off, the King of Hollywood
was paired with all of Hollywood's leading ladies. Adored by men as
well as women, in* Manhattan Melodrama *he plays a racketeer who
romances but finally loses Loy (to goodie-goodie William Powell).
In* Possessed, *he almost loses rough-around-the-edges Crawford,
whose real-life rough edges and animal magnetism fueled
an on-again, off-again 20-year torrid affair with the
one-time oil-rigger, lumberjack, and farmer.*

Clark Gable (with Joan Crawford)
STRANGE CARGO, 1940

Fresh from his stunning success in Gone with
the Wind, *Gable returned to the screen and his
favorite leading lady from the '30s (he hadn't
much cared for the high-brow and high-strung
Vivien Leigh) in this tale of sexual passion and
redemption. A half-hearted effort by MGM to
revive the failing fortunes of its former box-office
Queen, the film is fascinating as an example of
art imitating libido: the sexual chemistry between
the two stars was never more palpable.*

1117-7

Clark Gable (with Jean Harlow)
RED DUST, 1932

*"He treated her rough—and she loved it." Hollywood's original
he-man and the perfect foil for the studio's more refined romantic
leads, Gable made more money for MGM in the 1930s than
any other star. Paired with the tough-talking prostitute (Harlow)
in the risqué* Red Dust, *Gable met his sexual match, titillating
audiences and provoking moral crusaders around the country.*

Clark Gable (with Vivien Leigh)
GONE WITH THE WIND, 1939 (ABOVE)

Hollywood's most popular film of all time was the King's coronation ceremony—a synthesis of all of his previous cad-with-a-heart-of-gold roles. When Rhett plants a brutal kiss on bitch goddess Scarlett and later forces her further, the audience is solidly on his side. Gable was one man no woman could push around, even if, deep in our hearts, we really believed he <u>did</u> "give a damn."

Clark Gable (with Carole Lombard)
NO MAN OF HER OWN, 1932 (RIGHT)

A quintessentially Hollywood story of a heel reformed by the love of a good woman, No Man of Her Own *is most famous as the only celluloid pairing of Gable and Lombard, who were blissfully married seven years later. When the latter died tragically in a 1942 plane crash, tough-guy Gable broke down in the arms of erstwhile lover Joan Crawford, who had turned down his proposal of marriage earlier in their careers.*

Tyrone Power, 1938

The ultimate image of a male movie star, the pretty-boy scion of a respected acting dynasty was one of a handful of Twentieth Century-Fox's romantic leading men. Fresh from his biggest box-office hit, Lloyd's of London, *and on loan to MGM, Power is poised to star opposite Norma Shearer in that studio's incomparably resplendent (albeit overlong) historical production of* Marie Antoinette.

Errol Flynn (with Olivia de Havilland)

THE ADVENTURES OF ROBIN HOOD, 1938

The wicked, swashbuckling successor to Douglas Fairbanks,
the dashing, energetic Flynn reached the apogee of movie fame in
Robin Hood, *at the time of its release Warner Bros.' most expensive*
film to date. In real life a notorious womanizer ("in like Flynn"
gained national currency after the actor was accused and acquitted
of statutory rape in 1942), on-screen the Tasmanian-born devil
with the lithe body and infectious smile seduced women such as
Maid Marian (de Havilland) more by charm than brute force.
As high-spirited and rebellious on camera as off, the unapologetic
actor collapsed from too much fast living at the age of 50.

Nelson Eddy (with Jeannette MacDonald)

ROSE MARIE, 1936

In their most successful film collaboration, a Canadian Mountie
(Eddy) gets his man—and a woman (MacDonald)! America's
"singing sweethearts" were phenomenally popular with audiences in
the relatively innocent days preceding World War II. Concert stars
long before they garnered fame in Hollywood, the duo (known rudely
in some quarters as the Singing Capon and the Iron Butterfly) still
have a cult following today, their MGM operettas a fond reminder of
a sweetness that has long disappeared from motion pictures.

Burt Lancaster (with Ava Gardner)
THE KILLERS, 1946

*An overnight sensation as the brooding Swede and boy toy of
gangster moll Gardner in the low-budget, big-box-office hit*
The Killers, *the tall, athletic former acrobat and circus performer
from East Harlem almost single-handedly revived the swashbuckler
genre in the 1950s. No slouch as a romantic lead, Lancaster exuded
enough charisma and sex appeal to make his fiery pairing
with Gardner a film noir classic.*

Burt Lancaster (with Deborah Kerr)
FROM HERE TO ETERNITY, 1953 (ABOVE AND OVERLEAF)
*James Jones's seamy novel of army life during World War II
was much bowdlerized in the film adaptation. Dispensing
with the book's vulgar language and its frank indictment of the
U.S. military, the picture still packed a punch with Lancaster's
adulterous surfside rendezvous with costar Kerr,
one of the steamiest love scenes ever committed to celluloid.*

William Holden (with Gloria Swanson and Kim Novak)
SUNSET BOULEVARD, 1950 (ABOVE)
PICNIC, 1955 (RIGHT)

*Hollywood's ultimate parody of itself brought overnight acclaim to the former
William Franklin Beedle, Jr., the handsome, all-American son of a prominent
Pasadena businessman. If filmgoers had a hard time swallowing the romantic
entanglement of much-younger gigolo Holden and fading movie queen Swanson
(because Swanson, at 50, looked too good for her age, Holden's makeup was
changed to make him appear younger than his 32 years), they easily digested
the raw, animal attraction between Holden and costar Novak five years later
in* Picnic, *a sizzling hit that made the buxom, Columbia-manufactured
sex goddess the year's number one box-office draw.*

Paul Henreid (with Bette Davis)
NOW, VOYAGER, 1942

*A prototype of the continental lover, real-life aristocrat Henreid will
forever be remembered for the scene in the classic Warner Bros. tearjerker
when he lights two cigarettes simultaneously and hands one to Davis,
about as sexually suggestive as Hollywood got in the pre-rating days during
World War II. Released the same year as the less maudlin and even more
romantic Casablanca, in which the former Viennese stage actor
plays the gallant husband of Ingrid Bergman, Now, Voyager really belongs to
Davis, who, in her Jekyll-and-Hyde transformation from ugly duckling to
suffering-in-mink sophisticate, settles for the stars and a moment
of lovesick happiness with her knight in shining armor.*

John Garfield (with Lana Turner)

THE POSTMAN ALWAYS RINGS TWICE, 1946 (RIGHT)

In some ways a younger successor to Humphrey Bogart,
the former "Golden Boy" of New York's left-leaning Group Theatre
was a forerunner of the grittier, method-trained actors to emerge in
the 1950s. A drifter and rebel in real life, the one-time juvenile
delinquent brought a believable steam heat to his love scenes with
the wanton, all-in-white-clad Turner, underscoring a new kind of
sexual sensibility to emerge in post-war America.

John Wayne (with Claudette Colbert)

WITHOUT RESERVATIONS, 1946 (OVERLEAF)

Forever the rugged, ready-to-ride ideal of the American cowboy,
Wayne seemed to love his horses more than the women in his films.
But dressed in Marine uniform in this charming take-off on
the romantic comedy It Happened One Night, *the solid,*
six-feet-four-inch actor was convincing enough as a romantic lead,
especially playing against the ditsy charms of love-interest Colbert.
Not a box-office hit, the Mervyn LeRoy-directed comedy at least
showed that the true-grit star of over a hundred actioners
could win the West—<u>and</u> the girl.

Humphrey Bogart (with Ingrid Bergman and Lauren Bacall)

CASABLANCA, 1942 (ABOVE)

DARK PASSAGE, 1947 (RIGHT)

Incredibly, Hollywood's original tough-talking antihero, born into a wealthy social-register family and educated at Andover, spent much of his nascent career playing a variety of fops on the New York stage. Eventually typecast as a gangster, Bogart only found stardom in his forty-second year, in The Maltese Falcon. *Reluctant to play the romantic lead in* Casablanca *(Ronald Reagan was originally slated for the part!), the short, grizzled cynic gave the performance of a lifetime opposite Bergman in arguably the most romantic movie of all time. His subsequent collaboration (on-screen and off) with his future fourth wife, smoky ex-model Bacall, elevated Bogie forever to the pantheon of Hollywood's great lovers.*

Glenn Ford (with Rita Hayworth)
GILDA, 1946

*The stoic acting style of the all-American workhorse actor—
neither particularly handsome nor complex—provided a perfect foil
for many of Hollywood's more charismatic post-war leading ladies.
Relegated to mostly supporting roles in "B" pictures early in his
career, Ford was paired with Columbia's hottest property in the film
that made him a star and Hayworth a legend. When she does her
infamous striptease in a seedy, South American bar, we believe Ford
when he says: "There never was a woman like Gilda."*

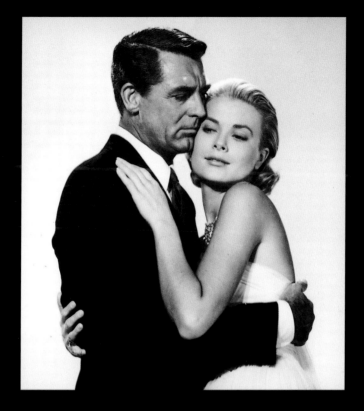

Cary Grant (with Ingrid Bergman and Grace Kelly)
To Catch a Thief, 1955 (ABOVE)
Notorious, 1946 (LEFT)

*The only romantic leading man who seemed to get better looking
with each passing year (he maintained a year-round suntan
to avoid wearing makeup), the self-invented, self-taught actor with
the unplaceable accent and sly wit made over seventy films before
suddenly retiring from show business to become the director of the
Fabergé cosmetics firm in 1966. Unsuccessful with women in real life
(all four of his wives left him), the elusive star seemed to be much
happier being chased from Monte Carlo to Rio on the big screen by
his glamorous Hitchcock costars Kelly and Bergman.*

James Dean (with Natalie Wood)
REBEL WITHOUT A CAUSE, 1955

The archetype of misunderstood Fifties youth, the brooding, sensitive
actor with only three credits to his name sparked with Rebel *a spate*
of troubled-youth films and garnered a cult following that has
not yet abated almost forty years after his tragic early death at
the age of twenty-four. Paired with seventeen-year-old Wood for
his second picture, Dean radiated a new kind of subtle sexuality,
so compressed it was explosive—perhaps explaining the "emotional
necrophilia" that followed the real-life rebel's demise.

Gregory Peck (with Audrey Hepburn)
ROMAN HOLIDAY, 1953
*The pairing of earnest, dependable Peck and waifish newcomer
Hepburn during an era when the movies were saturated with buxom
sex goddesses and sullen antiheroes was probably a stroke of genius.
Light, scenic, and magically comedic, the picture that garnered nine
Academy Award nominations (winning two, including Hepburn's
only Oscar, for Best Actress) was a breath of fresh air and a reminder
of the kinder, gentler romantic leads of yore.*

Anthony Perkins (with Sophia Loren)
DESIRE UNDER THE ELMS, 1958
*Two years before he would forever-after be known for his destructive
mother-fixation, the star of* Psycho *was fixated on his stern
New England father's bosomy Italian mail-order bride in this bizarre
adaptation of Eugene O'Neill's searing tale of familial lust and
treachery. Although Loren is generally miscast in the starring role,
her illicit seduction of the boyish Perkins is a moment of earthy
sexual tension rarely captured on film.*

Warren Beatty (with Natalie Wood)

SPLENDOR IN THE GRASS, 1961

The handsome, publicity-shy younger brother of Shirley MacLaine was an instant hit in his first Hollywood venture, yet another film in the rebellious-youth sex cycle popular at the time. While he and Wood forwent consummating their repressed sexual passion on-screen, off-screen the duo began a notorious love affair (breaking up Wood's marriage to actor Robert Wagner), the first of many for Hollywood's most prodigious modern-day lover.

65

Richard Burton (with Elizabeth Taylor)

CLEOPATRA, 1963

Called by Taylor "the most bizarre piece of entertainment ever to be perpetrated," this overwrought and outrageously expensive production was far more interesting for the brazen off-screen coupling of its two stars (wrecking Taylor's marriage to Eddie Fisher) than for the on-screen love story. Eventually married (and then divorced and remarried), Hollywood's insatiable violet-eyed love goddess and sometime home-wrecker and the ruggedly handsome miner's son from Wales appeared together in a string of self-involved, mostly forgettable films that were far more fascinating as reflections of the couple's on-again, off-again love affair than as works of serious art.

Ryan O'Neal (with Ali McGraw)

LOVE STORY, 1970

Proof that the theme of star-crossed love is one of Hollywood's most bankable formulas, this cliché-ridden update on the Romeo-and-Juliet theme is still one of the ten biggest box-office draws of all time. Turned down by no less than Jon Voight, Beau Bridges, Michael York, and Michael Douglas, the plum role of Oliver Barrett IV made the Oscar-nominated O'Neal, a former lifeguard and Peyton Place series regular, a film star and sex symbol overnight.

Omar Sharif (with Julie Christie)
DOCTOR ZHIVAGO, 1965 (RIGHT)

Inveterate gambler and champion bridge player, the dreamy-eyed son of a wealthy Egyptian merchant was a masterful lover as well, first as Egypt's leading romantic man in the 1950s (helped along by his marriage to that country's most popular actress) and afterward as an international movie star. In this gorgeously filmed if endless David Lean epic—billed as "a love caught in the fire of revolution"—Sharif and his exquisitely beautiful British costar seem more than willing to face the firing squad if they can make love just <u>one</u> more time.

Robert Redford (with Barbra Streisand)
THE WAY WE WERE, 1973 (OVERLEAF)

When opposites attract, there are bound to be sparks. And when Hollywood decided to pair its most popular fair-haired Adonis with everyone's favorite Funny Girl, there were enough on-screen fireworks for at least three movies. Although the love story of Katie and Hubbell is a variation of one of Tinseltown's oldest and most successful cinematic clichés, there was a new lesson to be learned in this three-handkerchief romantic tearjerker: opposites ultimately repel.

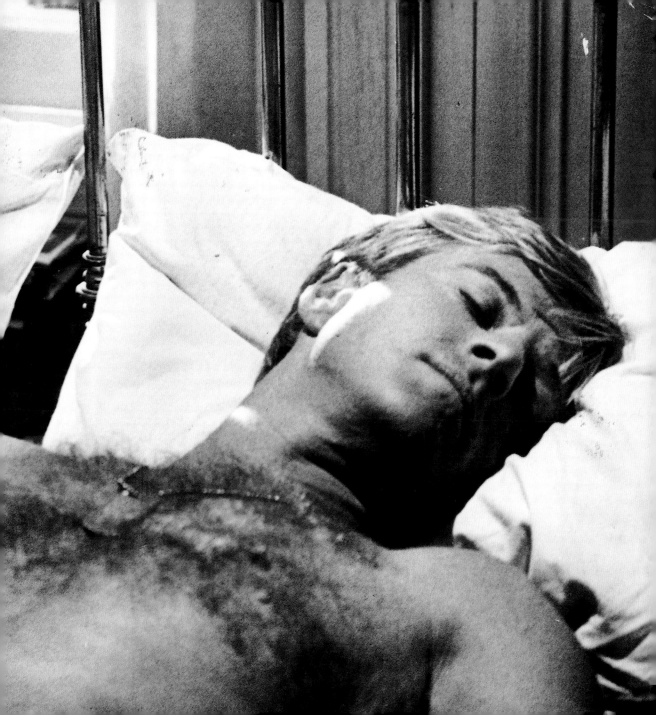

Kris Kristofferson (with Barbra Streisand)
A STAR IS BORN, 1976
*Country-western singer-songwriter, Rhodes Scholar, and former
West Point English teacher, handsome, raw-boned Renaissance man
Kristofferson still couldn't upstage La Streisand in this fourth remake
of the classic Hollywood chestnut. Critic Rex Reed's comment that
"to know her is not necessarily to love her" mirrored Streisand's
on-camera role as a driven singer who climbs her way to the top while
her marriage crumbles, her husband eventually killed in a car crash.
But when the box-office star and all-around diva sings the
Oscar-winning "Evergreen" at the end of the film, fans everywhere
fall in love with her all over again.*

Richard Gere (with Debra Winger)
AN OFFICER AND A GENTLEMAN, 1982

*Accused early in his career of acting more with his shirt (and pants!)
off than on, beefcake Gere played a number of rough types—from
street stud to gigolo—before becoming every woman's fantasy lover in
the box-office hit that became one of the most romantic films of the
1980s. Basically an old-fashioned story of love against the odds,
the somewhat predictable soap opera packed just enough nudity,
simulated sex, and profanity to titillate a more jaded audience and
guarantee true superstardom for the elusive Buddhist convert,
AIDS activist, and husband of top model Cindy Crawford.*

Jeremy Irons (with Meryl Streep)

THE FRENCH LIEUTENANT'S WOMAN, 1981

*A welcome throwback to the more elegant romantic leads of bygone
Hollywood, the classically trained British-born actor was paired with
America's premier actress in this ambitious cinematic rendering
of John Fowles's classic novel. Irons (fresh from his success in
Brideshead Revisited) gives a sexually explosive performance as
a Victorian gentleman torn between propriety and desire, proving
that a little old-fashioned repression goes a long way.*

78